S0-FQW-644

The New Glasses

By Paul Shipton

Illustrated by Fabiano Fiorin

Activities by Hannah Fish

Contents

OXFORD
UNIVERSITY PRESS

Hello! My name is Ben.
Hello! My name is Rosie.
This is Grandpa.
This is Grandpa's van. It's fantastic!

Ben
Rosie's brother

Rosie
Ben's sister

Grandpa

Clunk
Grandpa's robot

Max
Ben's friend

A boy in the playground

Now let's read this story, The New Glasses!

Ben and Max are in the school playground.

'Are you wearing new glasses?' Max asks.

'Yes,' says Ben. 'Do you like them?'

'They're very nice,' says Max.

Are you wearing new glasses?

Some boys are playing a game with a ball.

'Can we play, too?' Max asks them.

'OK,' says the boy with the ball.

Ben takes off his new glasses. 'I can't run and play in them,' he says.

→ Go to page 20 for activities.

The boy with the ball shouts, 'Catch!'

He throws the ball to Ben.

But Ben is putting his glasses in his pocket. The ball hits the glasses and they fall.

The boy runs to Ben. 'I'm sorry!'
he says.

'Are your new glasses OK?' Max asks.

Ben looks at the glasses. He is sad.

'No, look,' he says. 'They're broken!'

They're broken!

→ Go to page 21 for activities.

Ben has a bad day at school.

He sits down close to the board, but he can't see the numbers on it. His teacher writes a question, but Ben can't read it.

At four o'clock, Rosie sees Ben.

'Where are your new glasses?' she asks him.

Where are your new glasses?

Soon Grandpa and Clunk are here.

'Where are your new glasses, Ben?' asks Clunk.

Ben is very sad.

→ Go to page 22 for activities.

At home, Ben gets some tape and sits down at the table.

'What are you doing?' asks Rosie.

'I want to fix my glasses,' says Ben.

'You can't fix them with tape!'
says Grandpa.

Ben gives his broken glasses to
Grandpa. 'Can you fix them for me,
please?' he asks.

'No,' says Grandpa, 'but I can make
you some fantastic NEW glasses! I
can give them to you at breakfast.'

→ Go to page 23 for activities.

In the morning, Grandpa gives Ben his new glasses.

'Thanks, Grandpa!' says Ben.

Grandpa looks out the window. 'It's a sunny day,' he says. 'Let's ride our bikes to school today!'

'Great!' says Rosie.

Soon they are on their bikes. Max is there with his bike, too.

'Let's go!' says Grandpa. 'We can ride on the bike path.'

Ben is happy. He likes his new glasses.

Let's go!

Go to page 24 for activities.

They come to a bridge over a road.

A cat runs in front of them.

'Ben!' shouts Rosie. 'Don't hit that cat!'

Don't hit that cat!

Ben stops his bike, but
his new glasses fall.

'Oh no!' shouts Ben.

'Quick,' says Rosie. 'Get your glasses, Ben.'

But there is a strong wind. The glasses are on the bridge and then – oh no! – they fall onto the road under the bridge.

'Quick, Clunk!' Ben says. 'Please get them. A car's coming!'

Quick, Clunk!

→ Go to page 25 for activities.

But Clunk can't get the glasses.

Ben watches the car. It's coming at the glasses. The man in the car can't see them.

And then …

The car doesn't hit the glasses.

'They're OK!' says Max.

But there is a big yellow school bus on the road, too.

It doesn't go close to the glasses. It goes ON them.

'Oh no!' says Ben. 'Now they're broken, too!'

The glasses fly up.

→ Go to page 26 for activities.

'Catch them, Ben!' says Grandpa.

Ben looks up. He jumps with his hands out … and catches the glasses!

They're not broken!

Then he looks at them. 'They're NOT broken!'

'Grandpa makes fantastic, strong glasses,' says Clunk.

At school, the boys in the playground are playing with the ball again.

Ben looks at Max. 'Let's play!' he says.

Ben does not take off his glasses. He runs and shouts, 'Throw the ball to me!'

Throw the ball to me!

→ Go to page 27 for activities.

 **Activities** for pages 4–5

1 **Write the words.**

1 l y a p
play

2 k e t a   f o f

3 m e g a

4 a l b l

5 s e g s l a s

6 u n r

2 **Match.**

1 Ben and Max   playing with a ball.

2 Ben is wearing   off his new glasses.

3 Some boys are   are in the playground.

4 Ben takes   new glasses.

Talk **Do you play in the school playground?
What games do you play? Talk to a friend.**

Activities for pages 6–7

1 Circle the correct words.

1 A boy throws the ball **on** / **to** Ben.

2 The ball **hits** / **hitting** Ben's glasses.

3 The glasses **do fall** / **fall**.

4 Ben looks **of** / **at** the glasses.

5 Ben is **sadder** / **sad**.

6 His glasses **is** / **are** broken.

2 Put a tick (✓) or a cross (✗) in the box.

1 This is a ball. ☒

2 This is broken. ☐

3 This is a pocket. ☐

4 This is sad. ☐

 **Activities** for pages 8-9

1 Choose and write the correct words.

1 _____Ben_____ has a bad day at school. He sits close to the 2 _____, but he can't see the numbers on it. At four o'clock, Rosie sees Ben. Soon Grandpa and 3 _____ are here. Clunk says, 'Where are your new 4 _____, Ben?' Ben is very 5 _____.

school

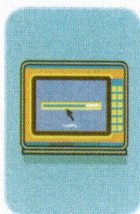
board

glasses

Clunk

Ben

falls

sad

catch

Talk **Do you wear glasses? Talk to a friend.**

1 Complete the sentences.

> tape ~~table~~ fix Grandpa make

1 Ben sits down at the ___table___ .

2 He wants to _____ his glasses.

3 But he can't fix them with _____ .

4 Ben gives his glasses to _____ .

5 Grandpa can _____ some new glasses.

**2 Look at the picture on page 10.
Write *yes* or *no*.**

1 Ben is sitting at the table. ___yes___

2 Rosie is sitting next to Ben. _____

3 Ben's glasses are on the table. _____

4 Ben's glasses are red. _____

5 There is some tape on the table. _____

6 Rosie has green glasses. _____

7 Grandpa is eating breakfast. _____

 **Activities** for pages 12–13

1 Match.

1 happy

2 ride

3 window

4 sunny

5 bike path

6 bike

2 Look at the picture on page 13. Answer the questions.

1 How many bikes are there? _____three_____

2 What color is Ben's bike? _____

3 Is Clunk on a bike? _____

4 How many trees are there? _____

Talk **Do you have a bike? Talk to a friend.**

Activities for pages 14–15

1 Write the words.

1 r e g b i d

_____

2 r g t o n s

_____

3 t c a

_____

4 v r e o

_____

5 d o a r

_____

6 r u d n e

_____

2 Order the words.

1 runs / of them. / A cat / in front

<u>A cat runs in front of them.</u>

2 his glasses / Ben stops / his bike, / fall. / but

_____

3 is / wind. / There / strong / a

_____

4 under / fall / Ben's glasses / the bridge.

_____

✿ **Activities** for pages 16–17

1 **Put a tick (✓) or a cross (✗) in the box.**

1 This is a car. ☐

2 This is a man. ☐

3 This is a school bus. ☐

4 This is yellow. ☐

2 **Look at the picture at the bottom of page 17.**
Write *yes* or *no*.

1 A school bus is on the road. _____

2 There is a cat on the road. _____

3 Ben and Rosie are on the bridge. _____

4 Ben is happy. _____

5 Clunk is on the school bus. _____

1 Circle the correct words.

1 Ben jumps with **his** / **he's** hands out.

2 Ben **catches** / **catch** the glasses.

3 The glasses are **no** / **not** broken.

4 Grandpa makes **strongest** / **strong** glasses.

2 Choose and write the correct words.

Ben ¹ _____ and catches the glasses.

He looks at the glasses. They are not

² _____! The glasses are very strong.

In the school playground, Ben plays with

the ³ _____ again. Now he does not

⁴ _____ his glasses!

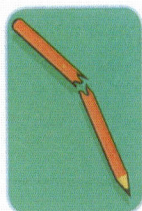    

broken   throws   jumps   take off   ball

Talk **Do you like this story? Talk to a friend.**

Story Characters

1 Write the names.

Clunk

_____ _____

_____ _____

2 Write about these characters.

Ben _wears red glasses._

Rosie _____

Grandpa _____

Clunk _____

3 Now draw a new character.

Name:

4 Write about your new character.

_____

_____

_____

Talk The characters are the people in a story. Who is your favorite character in this story? Talk to a friend.

ball

bike

bike path

breakfast

bridge

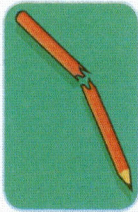
broken

car

cat

catch

fall

fix

game

glasses

hit

in front of

make

over

play

playground

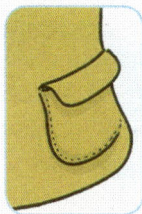
pocket

ride

road

sad

school bus

shout

strong

sunny

take off

tape

teacher

throw

under

Oxford Read and Imagine

Oxford Read and Imagine graded readers are at nine levels (Early Starter, Starter, Beginner, and Levels 1 to 6) for students from age 3 to 4 and older. They offer great stories to read and enjoy.

Activities provide Cambridge Young Learner Exams preparation. See Key below.

At Levels 1 to 6, every storybook reader links to an **Oxford Read and Discover** non-fiction reader, giving students a chance to find out more about the world around them, and an opportunity for Content and Language Integrated Learning (CLIL).

For more information about **Read and Imagine**, and for Teacher's Notes, go to www.oup.com/elt/teacher/readandimagine

KEY | **S** Activity supports Cambridge Young Learner Starters Exam preparation

Oxford Read and Discover

Do you want to find out more about eyes, and how people and animals protect their eyes? You can read this non-fiction book.

Eyes

OXFORD
UNIVERSITY PRESS

Great Clarendon Street, Oxford, OX2 6DP, United Kingdom

Oxford University Press is a department of the University of Oxford. It furthers the University's objective of excellence in research, scholarship, and education by publishing worldwide. Oxford is a registered trade mark of Oxford University Press in the UK and in certain other countries

Enquiries concerning reproduction outside the scope of the above should be sent to the ELT Rights Department, Oxford University Press, at the address above

You must not circulate this work in any other form and you must impose this same condition on any acquirer

Links to third party websites are provided by Oxford in good faith and for information only. Oxford disclaims any responsibility for the materials contained in any third party website referenced in this work

ISBN: 978 0 19 470930 9

Printed in China

This book is printed on paper from certified and well-managed sources

ACKNOWLEDGEMENTS

Main illustrations by: Fabiano Fiorin/Milan Illustrations Agency.

Additional illustrations by: Dusan Pavlic/Beehive illustration, Alan Rowe, Mark Ruffle.